THE FINAL FRONTIER

BY JOHN HAMILTON

John Hamilton

VISIT US AT

WWW.ABDOPUBLISHING.COM

Published by ABDO Publishing Company, 4940 Viking Drive, Suite 622, Edina, Minnesota 55435.

Printed in the United States.

Editor: Paul Joseph
Graphic Design: John Hamilton
Cover Design: Neil Klinepier
Cover Illustration: *Under Fire* ©1980 Janny Wurts
Interior Photos and Illustrations: p 1 Starship Enterprise, Corbis; p 4 *Under Fire* ©1980 Janny Wurts;
p 5 *Starship's Trooper* ©1977 Don Maitz; p 6 *Planet Comics*; p 7 *Strong Arm Tactics* ©2003 Don Maitz; p
8 *Star Wars* lobby poster, courtesy 20th Century Fox; p 9 *New Sun*, ©1998 Don Maitz; p 10 (top) "Grey
Lensman," *Astounding Science Fiction*; p 10 (bottom) spaceship by Anton Brzezinski, Corbis; p 11 "Second
Stage Lensmen," *Astounding Science Fiction*; p 12 *Captain Future*, by Anton Brzezinski, Corbis;
p 14 (top) Leigh Bracket and Edmond Hamilton; p 14 (bottom) *The Long Tomorrow*, courtesy Ballantine
Books; p 15 (top) *The Secret of Sinharat*, courtesy Ace Books; p 15 (bottom) *The Empire Strikes Back* lobby
poster, courtesy 20th Century Fox; p 16 Buster Crabbe as Buck Rogers, Corbis; p 17 montage painting
of *Buck Rogers in the 25th Century*, Corbis; p 18 (top) Flash Gordon comic book, courtesy King Comics;
p 18 (bottom) Zarkov, Dale, and Flash, Corbis; p 19 poster for Flash Gordon movie, Corbis; p 20 (top)
William Shatner as Captain Kirk, Corbis; p 20 (bottom) Starship *Enterprise* vs. Klingon ship, courtesy
Paramount Television; p 21 (top) cast of *Star Trek*, Corbis; p 21 (bottom) Brent Spiner as Data, Corbis;
p 22 lobby poster for *Dune*, courtesy Universal Pictures; p 23 cover of Frank Herbert's *Dune*, courtesy
Orion Publishing Group; p 24 (top) X-wings from *Star Wars*, courtesy 20th Century Fox; p 24 (bottom)
Revenge of the Sith lobby poster, courtesy 20th Century Fox; p 25 Darth Vader, Corbis; p 26 Spaceships
attack planet, Corbis; p 27 Astronaut opens door, Corbis; p 28 *Pushing Ice*, courtesy Orion Publishing
Group; p 29 (top) *Hyperion*, courtesy Orion Publishing Group; p 29 (bottom) Dan Simmons, Corbis.

Library of Congress Cataloging-in-Publication Data

Hamilton, John, 1959-
    The final frontier / John Hamilton.
        p. cm. -- (The world of science fiction)
    Includes index.
    ISBN-13: 978-1-59679-987-5
    ISBN-10: 1-59679-987-0
    1. Science fiction--History and criticism--Juvenile literature. 2. Science fiction films--History and
criticism--Juvenile literature. I. Title. II. Series: Hamilton, John, 1959- World of science fiction.

PN3433.5.H35 2007
809.3'8762--dc22
                                    2006016395

CONTENTS

SPACE OPERA

Spaceships hurtling through the galaxy. Robots. Evil emperors. Laser guns. Space battles. Heroes and villains, princesses, rogues, and aliens. These are some of the ingredients of "space opera," a popular flavor of science fiction that emphasizes bold characters, a gee-whiz sense of wonder, and non-stop action and adventure.

Space opera is the kind of story most people think of when they hear the words "science fiction." It's especially popular today, both in books and movies. Space opera usually takes place on distant planets, with starships that can quickly travel between the stars. This is unrealistic, but it keeps the story fast-paced. *Star Trek* and *Star Wars* are examples of modern space opera, with larger-than-life heroes exploring strange new worlds and battling evil galactic empires in galaxies far, far away.

The term "space opera" is a combination of "soap opera" and "horse opera" (Westerns), which are both common types of drama with simple characters and predictable stories. (Ironically, none of these fiction genres has anything to do with singing.) Many people who grew up after the mid-1970s are surprised to learn that space opera was once frowned upon. It was considered a "lesser" form of science fiction.

Starting in the 1920s, when modern science fiction first became popular, many stories were published in cheap magazines called "pulps." The public's appetite for science fiction was ravenous. Countless magazines, with names like *Amazing Stories, Air Wonder Stories,* and *Astounding Science Fiction,* filled the newsstands. Some of the most popular stories were those of E. E. "Doc" Smith and his *Lensman* series, or the space adventure tales of Edmond Hamilton and Leigh Brackett.

Facing page: Starship's Trooper, by Don Maitz. *Below: Under Fire,* by Janny Wurts.

The best of these stories explored how science would affect the future of mankind, but the main appeal was the wild action and sense of wonder. As the years passed, in order to fill their magazines month after month, desperate editors often published stories that used tired themes and clichéd, one-dimensional characters. It was the same old stuff that readers had seen time and again. By the 1930s and early 1940s, science fiction was riddled with this kind of bad writing. Shining gems of originality were certainly printed, but all too often publishers took the easy way out, sticking with still more stories of fearless spacemen traveling to alien planets, rescuing damsels in distress. These "formulaic" stories were as predictable as many popular Westerns of the time, but instead of shooting from the hip with Colt .45's, the heroes used ray guns. There were also similarities to sea adventure stories, or tales of pirates, or exploration of unknown Africa, all of which were very popular in the first half of the 20th century.

Facing page: Strong Arm Tactics, by Don Maitz. *Below:* The cover of the May, 1941, issue of *Planet Comics.*

These kinds of stories also found their way into comic books, including *Planet Comics* of the 1940s. Movies and, later, television soon followed the same formula. Audiences (especially teenage boys) swooned over heroes such as Buck Rogers, Flash Gordon, Captain Video, and Tom Corbett, Space Cadet.

Wilson Tucker, a popular mystery and science fiction author, may have been the first to use the term "space opera." In 1941, he wrote an essay about bad science fiction. Tucker said, "In these hectic days of phrase-coining, we offer one. Westerns are called 'horse opera,' the morning tear-jerkers are called 'soap operas.' For the hacky, grinding, stinking, outworn space-ship yarn, or world-saving for that matter, we offer 'space opera.'"

By the 1950s and early 1960s, space opera stories were thoroughly scorned, their reputation in tatters. "Hard science fiction" reigned supreme, with its roots grounded in reality. These stories were about science, first and foremost. It was an insult to be labeled "space opera." In the 1960s, a new type of science fiction emerged called "New Wave." These stories attempted to bring science fiction into the mainstream, with an emphasis on literary excellence and a concern for style. Moving even further away from space opera, writers such as Harlan Ellison and Michael Moorcock experimented with stories about psychology, sociology, and the nature of humankind.

Lost in all this "literary" science fiction was a sense of wonder and adventure. In the late 1970s and early 1980s, space opera became popular again. People who grew up reading the early tales of planetary escapades became nostalgic. Space opera stories were remembered fondly—they represented the good-old-days of science fiction. At the same time, a new generation of writers and filmmakers began creating science fiction adventure stories. They didn't think of space opera as a low art form, which only hacks would stoop to create. Instead, these writers breathed fresh air into the genre. They proved that good writing and scientific ideas could exist alongside popular entertainment. This new, or postmodern, space opera is often artistic and thought provoking, all wrapped in an exciting adventure story.

Star Wars, Star Trek, Farscape, Andromeda… space opera seems to be everywhere nowadays. It's the kind of science fiction people turn to when they want to be entertained. Space opera is colorful, larger-than-life, with stalwart heroes and wicked villains battling in the far reaches of outer space.

Facing page: New Sun, by Don Maitz. *Below:* A lobby poster for *Star Wars.*

E.E. SMITH

Above: "Grey Lensman" in *Astounding Science Fiction.*
Below: A spaceship.

More than any other writer, E. E. "Doc" Smith (1890-1965) was responsible for inventing space opera. He is most famous for his *Lensman* and *Skylark* series of novels from the 1930s and 1940s, even though he continued publishing well into the 1960s. His novels featured intergalactic intrigue and non-stop action.

Edward Elmer Smith was born on May 2, 1890, in Wisconsin, but he grew up in Washington and Idaho. He studied chemistry in college, and received a doctorate in chemical engineering in 1917, which is why he often went by the nickname, "Doc."

Many consider Doc Smith's six *Lensman* books to be the greatest space opera ever written. The language seems a little dated and flowery by today's standards, but when they were published in the 1930s and 1940s, the *Lensman* books were groundbreaking.

Spanning millions of years and several galaxies, complete with rocketships, aliens, and interstellar warfare, the books tell the story of a group of space policemen called the Lensmen. In a galaxy-wide war between two powerful alien races, carefully chosen people (and aliens) join the Galactic Patrol to battle the forces of evil. They wear a special "Lens" on their skin, which allows them to read minds and communicate with any living being.

The *Lensman* books were very successful. Smith invented many science fiction concepts that are commonplace today, such as having aliens as major characters, and strong, competent women instead of mere damsels in distress. Other publishers rushed to follow Smith's formula, imitating the books so much that the science fiction category of space opera was born.

Above: "Second Stage Lensmen" in the November, 1941, issue of *Astounding Science Fiction.*

Unlike most of the imitators, however, the *Lensman* books were not simple fantasies. Smith took care to keep the science in his stories as real as possible. At the time, his books were called "super-science" stories. As the expression "space opera" became more common, Smith's imitators gradually discarded most of the science elements, emphasizing predictable action and adventure instead, and dooming space opera to the literary gutter for years to come.

EDMOND HAMILTON

Along with E. E. "Doc" Smith, Edmond Hamilton (1904-1977) is most often considered one of the original creators of space opera. He started his writing career with a short story called "The Monster God of Mamurth," published in *Weird Tales* magazine in 1926. He then went on to publish hundreds of short stories and dozens of novels, starting with the pulp magazines of the 1930s and 1940s. His career spanned several decades, and included detective stories as well as science fiction. He was one of the few authors to start in the early pulp magazine days of science fiction and continue through the post-nuclear Cold War era of the 1960s.

Hamilton's space opera stories earned him the nickname of "World Wrecker." Many of his stories were about evil menaces that threatened all life in the galaxy. The villains were often defeated by fleets of spaceships, and many worlds were blown up in the process.

One of Hamilton's most popular creations were his *Captain Future* stories, which were published in the pulp magazines from 1940 to 1951. Captain Future is the alias of Curtis Newton, a brilliant scientist who travels throughout the solar system, helping people and fighting evil. His companions include a robot named Grag, an android named Otho, and a fellow scientist whose brain is suspended in a floating glass case.

Several elements of the *Captain Future* tales can be seen reflected in *Star Wars* and its sequels. George Lucas, creator of *Star Wars*, was a big fan of Edmond Hamilton's writing. Hamilton's robots, Grag and Otho, bicker a lot, just like R2-D2 and C-3PO from *Star Wars*. Hamilton's characters also used "energy swords," similar to the familiar light saber of the Jedi Knights.

In 1946, Hamilton married fellow science fiction author Leigh Brackett, another pioneer of space opera tales.

Facing page:
A painting
of Edmond
Hamilton's *Captain*
Future, by artist
Anton Brzezinski.

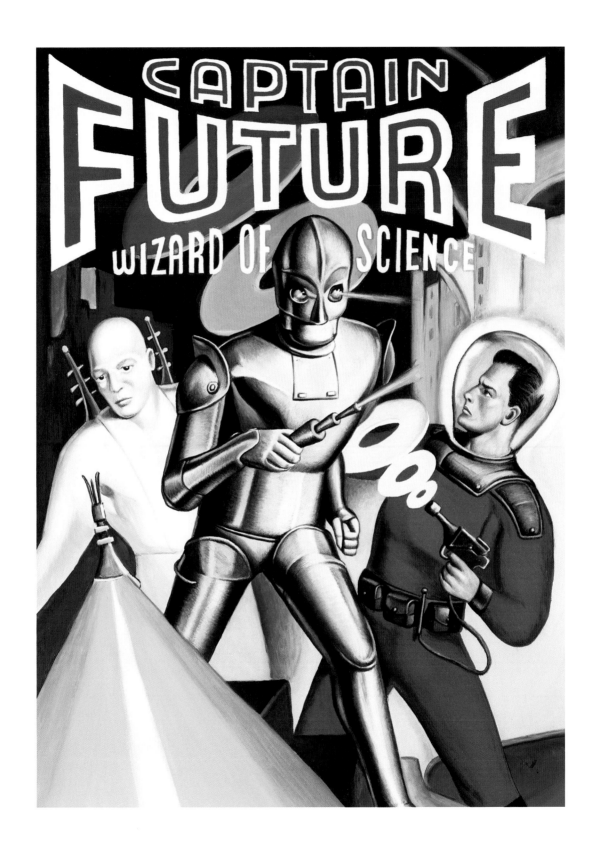

LEIGH BRACKETT

Above: Leigh Brackett with husband Edmond Hamilton.

Leigh Brackett (1915-1978) grew up in Southern California. She was an athletic kid who also loved reading the adventure stories of Edgar Rice Burroughs. Brackett eventually decided to write her own tales of space adventure. Her first science fiction story, "Martian Quest," was published in 1940 in *Astounding Science Fiction.* She continued writing science fiction, but she was also an accomplished author of mystery novels. She also worked in Hollywood as a screenwriter. In 1946, she co-wrote the script for *The Big Sleep,* starring Humphrey Bogart.

Bracket married science fiction author Edmond Hamilton in 1946. She was a positive influence on Hamilton's writing. People noticed that his *Captain Future* characters became more interesting after he married Bracket.

Leigh Brackett continued writing science fiction well into the 1970s. *The Long Tomorrow,* published in 1955, is a mature sci fi thriller about a post-apocalypse America. Some consider it her masterpiece. But it's her pulp magazine fiction of the 1940s for which she may be remembered most. This earlier work was pure fun: fast-paced, planet-hopping,

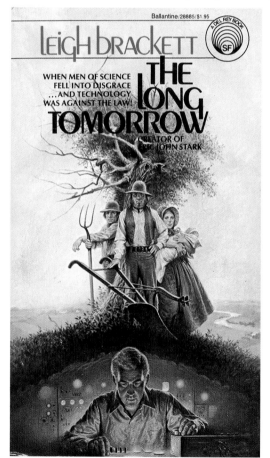

Left: Some people consider Leigh Brackett's *The Long Tomorrow* to be her science fiction masterpiece.

laser-blasting space opera. Her stories included such ripping yarns as *The Stellar Legion, Water Pirates, The Dragon Queen of Venus,* and *Outpost on Io.* She even wrote a story with the help of science fiction giant Ray Bradbury, called *Lorelei of the Red Mist.*

Like E. E. "Doc" Smith and Edmond Hamilton, Leigh Brackett wrote stories that were the best kind of space opera. They were wild adventures, but were still rooted in scientific possibility. For example, in the 1930s and 1940s, many astronomers guessed that Mars was a dry planet that may once have been inhabited by an ancient race of aliens; Venus was probably a cloudy, rainy jungle world. Leigh Brackett's stories reflected these scientific "facts," even though today we know they are untrue. But in keeping with the facts as they were known at the time, her stories had an air of believability, as well as being great adventures.

As the decades went by, Brackett continued writing science fiction, as well as mysteries and screenplays. Shortly before her death in 1978, she wrote a screenplay for the first *Star Wars* sequel, *The Empire Strikes Back.* She received screen credit for her work, along with screenwriter Lawrence Kasdan. Many critics think *The Empire Strikes Back* is the best of the *Star Wars* films, thanks in part to Brackett's writing. In 1981, for her work on the screenplay, she was posthumously given the Hugo Award, science fiction's highest honor.

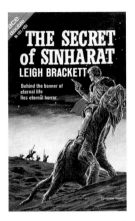

Above: The Secret of Sinharat, a novel by Leigh Brackett.

Left: Leigh Brackett received a Hugo Award for her work on the screenplay of *The Empire Strikes Back.*

BUCK ROGERS

Buck Rogers was a very popular space opera hero of the early 20th century. He first appeared in Philip Francis Nowlan's 1928 novella titled, *Armageddon 2419 A.D.*, which was published in *Amazing Stories* magazine. The hero, Anthony "Buck" Rogers, gets trapped in a cave and falls unconscious due to a mysterious radioactive gas. He wakes up 500 years later, in the 25th century, and then proceeds to save Earth from the forces of evil. A sequel, *The Airlords of Han*, was published in 1929.

Buck Rogers in the 25th Century debuted as the world's first science fiction comic strip in August 1929. It was extremely popular, running continuously for 38 years in more than 400 newspapers around the world. In 1932, Buck Rogers broke new ground once again, debuting in a radio serial on CBS that aired for 15 years. Both the comic strip and radio show featured what people came to call "that Buck Rogers stuff": death rays, missiles, spaceships, robots, and more.

In 1939, Hollywood launched a 12-part Buck Rogers movie serial, starring Buster Crabbe. The plot was similar to the earlier Buck Rogers stories, except in this version Buck and his companion, Buddy, are frozen for 500 years after a terrible dirigible accident in the Arctic. They are awoken by scientists in the year 2440, and then enlisted to help rid the world of its evil ruler, Killer Kane, and his super-gangsters.

Buck Rogers remained a well-liked space opera hero through the years, eventually starring in two television series, video games, board games, and several paperback novels and graphic novels.

FLASH GORDON

Above: A Flash Gordon comic book.

Facing page: A poster for a Flash Gordon movie.

Below, from left to right: Dr. Zarkov, Dale, and Flash.

"World coming to end! Strange new planet rushing toward Earth! Only miracle can save us… "

Flash Gordon was a popular space opera hero of the 1930s and 1940s. He eventually went on to have his own U.S. postage stamp, and was part of the inspiration for George Lucas's *Star Wars* movies.

Flash Gordon started as a comic strip in 1934. First drawn by legendary comic artist Alex Raymond, the strip was created by King Features Syndicate in order to compete against the successful *Buck Rogers* comic strips.

The Flash Gordon story begins when astronomers detect a mysterious planet on a collision course for Earth. Adventurer Flash Gordon, his companion Dale Arden, and the brilliant Dr. Hans Zarkov take off in the scientist's rocketship to intercept the mysterious threat. They crash-land on Mongo (the new planet's name). The impact jars Mongo into a new orbit, sparing Earth, but Flash, Dale, and Zarkov are stranded. They discover that Mongo is inhabited by a number of strange alien races, all of who suffer under the evil rule of Ming the Merciless.

In the forest-nation of Arboria, Flash becomes friends with exiled Prince Barin, the rightful heir to the throne. In a series of wild adventures across Mongo, Flash, Dale, and Zarkov join forces with Barin to battle the tyrant Ming.

The Flash Gordon comics were so popular that three movies were produced, each starring Buster Crabbe: *Flash Gordon* (1936), *Flash Gordon's Trip to Mars* (1938), and *Flash Gordon Conquers the Universe* (1940). A television series was produced in the 1950s, as well as an animated series in 1979. In 1980, another movie was produced. This version was simply called *Flash Gordon*, and starred Sam J. Jones as Flash, and Max von Sydow as Ming the Merciless.

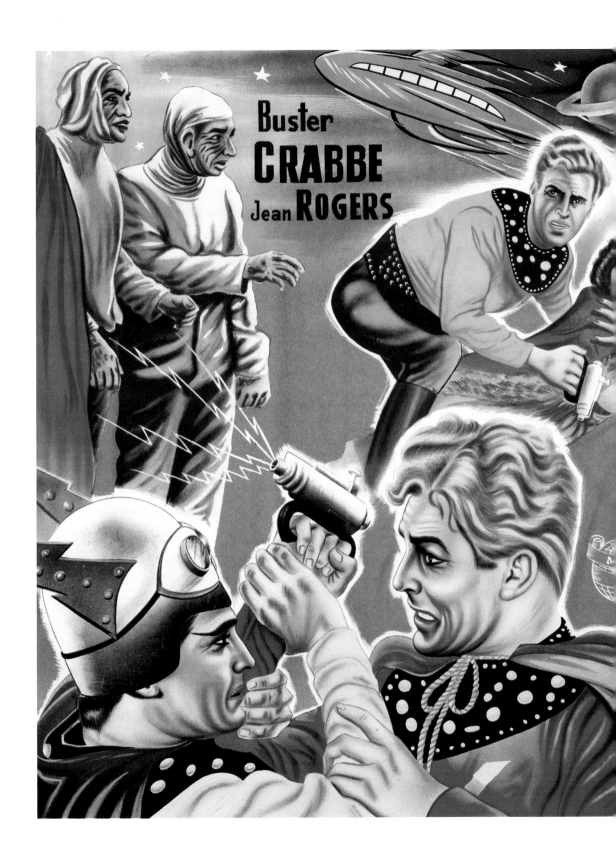

STAR TREK

Above: William Shatner as Captain James T. Kirk.

Below: The starship *Enterprise* faces off against a Klingon battlecruiser.

"...to boldly go where no one has gone before."

When the starship *Enterprise* first zoomed across television screens on September 8, 1966, producer Gene Roddenberry had no idea how big a phenomenon he had created. His show was called *Star Trek*. It was an ambitious, yet low-budget, science fiction adventure series. From this small beginning, *Star Trek* grew into a cherished show that eventually included five different live-action television series, an animated series, ten feature films, plus hundreds of novels, short stories, and video games.

The original *Star Trek* series ran for three seasons in the late 1960s, for a total of 79 episodes. Each show centered on the crew of the United Federation of Planets starship *USS Enterprise* NCC-1701. The 23rd-century adventurers included Captain James T. Kirk, Chief Medical Officer Leonard McCoy, and the ship's science officer, Mr. Spock, an alien from the planet Vulcan. Together with a cast of colorful supporting characters, they traveled the galaxy exploring strange, new worlds.

Gene Roddenberry promoted the show as a sort of Western in outer space, a classic space opera. Roddenberry had an optimistic, utopian vision of the future, where problems such as racism, sexism, and poverty, were things of the past. The crew of the *Enterprise* represented all races and genders (it even had an alien—Mr. Spock—as a major character). It was a daring move for a 1960s television show.

Star Trek wasn't immediately successful. But after it went into reruns, devoted fan support grew steadily. In 1979, the original cast returned for another voyage, in *Star Trek: The Motion Picture*. The film was a hit. It was followed by nine other features, with more on the way.

In 1987, a new *Star Trek* came to television. *Star Trek: The Next Generation*

featured a completely new cast, with a storyline that takes place a century after the original *Star Trek*. A huge hit with fans, the show lasted for seven seasons. Other spin-offs followed, including *Star Trek: Deep Space Nine*, *Star Trek: Voyager*, and *Star Trek: Enterprise*.

Above: The cast of the original *Star Trek* series, from left to right: James Doohan, DeForest Kelley, Walter Koenig, Majel Barrett, William Shatner, Nichelle Nichols, Leonard Nimoy, and George Takei.

Left: Brent Spiner, as the android Lieutenant Commander Data, from *Star Trek: The Next Generation*.

DUNE

Dune is a sprawling space opera that many consider one of the finest science fiction novels ever written. The story takes place in the far future, on the desert planet of Arrakis, also called Dune. Paul Atreides and his royal family move to Dune and become involved in a complex tale of political intrigue, culture clashes, and the fate of the galaxy, with a heavy emphasis on ecology and religion. Paul Atreides eventually becomes a hero who leads the desert people of Dune and overthrows the evil empire.

Facing page: A cover from an edition of Frank Herbert's novel, *Dune.* *Below:* A lobby poster for the 1984 movie version of *Dune.*

First published in 1965, *Dune* won both the Hugo and Nebula Awards, science fiction's top honors. The book has sold more than 20 million copies, and it has been translated into dozens of languages, making it one of the best-selling science fiction novels ever. It was also turned into a movie in 1984. A television mini-series aired in 2000 on the Sci Fi Channel.

Dune's author was Frank Herbert. Born in 1920, in Tacoma, Washington, he knew early on what he wanted to be when he grew up. On his eighth birthday, he stood on the kitchen table and declared to his family, "I want to be an author!" Herbert was very smart, and curious about the world around him. But his independent streak often got him in trouble. He never graduated from college because he only wanted to study what interested him.

It took six years for Herbert to write *Dune.* It was rejected by 23 publishers before it was serialized in *Analog* magazine. After *Dune's* smashing success, Herbert wrote five sequels set in the same fictional universe.

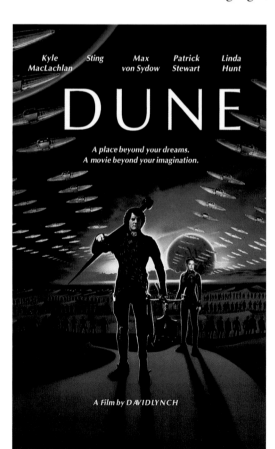

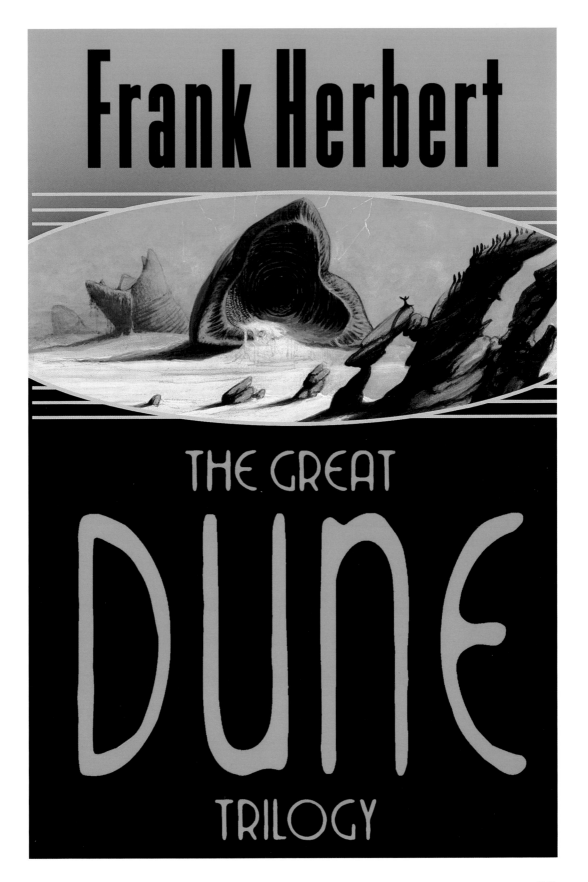

Frank Herbert

THE GREAT

DUNE

TRILOGY

STAR WARS

Above: A space battle scene from *Star Wars.*
Below: A lobby poster for *Star Wars: Episode III - Revenge of the Sith.*

"A long time ago in a galaxy far, far away…"

In the 1970s, producer/director George Lucas wanted to film a remake of *Flash Gordon.* Lucas loved space opera, especially the old-time stories from the 1930s and 1940s. But the rights to *Flash Gordon* were already taken. Lucas decided to write his own story. In 1977, *Star Wars* entered movie theaters with a supernova of critical praise and fan enthusiasm.

Star Wars may be the best modern example of space opera ever created. It is an action-packed thrill ride with all the elements of a good old-fashioned space adventure: planet-hopping rocketships, robots, blasters, evil emperors, political intrigue, Imperial stormtroopers, larger-than-life heroes, and even a bit of mysticism thrown in for good measure. ("May the Force be with you.")

Star Wars tells the story of Luke Skywalker, a farmboy from the small backwater planet of Tatooine. He rises to the rank of Jedi Knight in a quest to aid the Rebel Alliance against his arch nemesis, Darth Vader, and the evil forces of the Galactic Empire. Luke teams up with several other characters, including his mentor, Jedi Knight Obi-Wan Kenobi, plus Princess Leia, Chewbacca, and smuggler Han Solo. Two robots, called droids, are also major characters: the no-nonsense, trash-can shaped R2-D2, and the quirky, vain, gold-plated C-3PO.

Star Wars was so popular that George Lucas soon produced two sequels, *The Empire Strikes Back* (1980), and *Return of the Jedi* (1983). In 1999, Lucas released *The Phantom Menace,* a "prequel" to the first three movies. Two other movies followed: *Attack of the Clones* (2002), and *Revenge of the Sith* (2005). Together, these three films explain the rise of the Galactic Empire, and the story of how Anakin Skywalker (Luke's father) became a Jedi Knight, and was then corrupted by the Dark Side of the Force to become Darth Vader.

Below: Darth Vader leads a group of Imperial stormtroopers into battle.

NEW SPACE OPERA

Space opera is as popular as ever—the *Star Wars* films are proof of that, with nearly $20 billion dollars in ticket sales, home videos, games, toys, and novels. But as a category of science fiction, the genre is gradually changing. Starting in the mid 1970s, and gaining strength ever since, "new" space opera is cracking the mold.

Facing page: An astronaut opens the door to a new universe.
Below: Spaceships attack an alien city in this painting by Anton Brzezinski.

Space opera seems to be a little darker now. Readers are often uncertain if the protagonist (the main subject of the book) is a "good guy" or a "bad guy." This might be an influence of the cyberpunk movement of the 1980s, which featured anti-heroes who fought against established society. Space opera stories with messages like "good over evil" or "the success of mankind," are too simple nowadays. Instead, new space opera focuses on complex, fully developed characters, with intricate plots. Newer technologies, such as those used in space travel, are often described in great detail. This attention to accuracy and scientific plausibility is similar to what is found in "hard" science fiction. And yet, new space opera keeps one foot in its old traditions: stories happen on a grand scale, spanning galaxies and centuries. A sense of wonder is still a requirement for good space opera.

Right: The cover to Alastair Reynolds' novel, *Pushing Ice*.

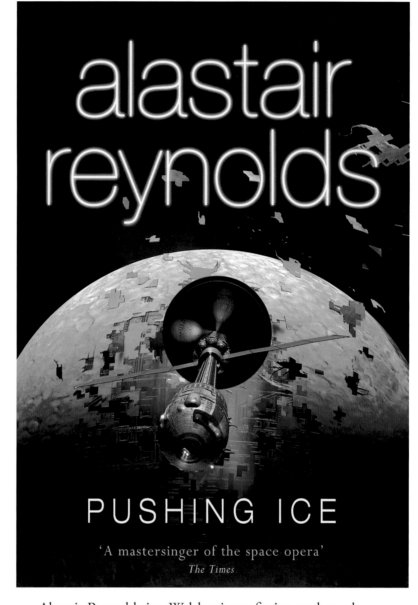

Alastair Reynolds is a Welsh science fiction author who produces this new kind of space opera. Before becoming a writer, he was a physicist and astronomer. His books reflect his scientific background. His *Revelation Space* series of stories, which span several hundred years, feature technology that would logically work based on our understanding of science today—a hallmark of hard science fiction.

In 1989, Dan Simmons published *Hyperion*, a Hugo Award-winning novel set in the far future. A group of pilgrims travels across the planet Hyperion on their way to a remote valley filled with mysterious Time Tombs. Along the way, the travelers confront the Shrike, a huge four-armed, razor-and-spike covered god-machine whose purpose is to create pain and suffering.

During their journey, each traveler relates his or her own intertwining story, much like the *Canterbury Tales* by 14th century author Geoffrey Chaucer. Other literary references abound, such as 19th century poet John Keats. (The title *Hyperion* refers to one of Keats's poems.)

Simmons continued his saga in 1990 with *The Fall of Hyperion*. Two more books followed, *Endymion* (1996) and *The Rise of Endymion* (1997). Taken together, these four books are called the *Hyperion Cantos*.

Dan Simmons masterfully weaved many complex themes into this epic series, yet the books are also spellbinding tales of adventure. The scientific details are utterly believable, but it is the human drama that is most memorable. Simmons's characters are fascinating and multi-dimensional. These are not simple *Buck Rogers* or *Flash Gordon* whiz-bang stories—they represent the new face of space opera.

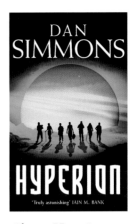

Above: Hyperion, a novel by Dan Simmons.

Below: Author Dan Simmons.

GLOSSARY

ANDROID
A kind of robot that mimics people, both in appearance and behavior. In Edmond Hamilton's *Captain Future* stories, Otho is a type of android.

APOCALYPSE
An apocalypse is a catastrophe that causes complete destruction on a worldwide scale. Post-apocalypse is a common type of science fiction. "Post" means "after." Post-apocalypse science fiction shows what kind of society would arise after a global disaster.

CLONE
An organism that is "grown" from donor cells, making an exact copy of the original.

COLD WAR
The mainly diplomatic conflict waged between the United States and the former Soviet Union after World War II. The Cold War resulted in a large buildup of weapons and troops. It ended when the Soviet Union broke up in the late 1980s and early 1990s.

CYBERPUNK
The word cyberpunk is a combination of the words punk and cybernetics, which is the science of control and communication of both machines and living creatures. Originally, it was meant to describe antisocial rebels who use computers to commit their crimes. Nowadays, cyberpunk more commonly refers to a tech-savvy hero who fights back, using the system against itself.

GALAXY
A system of millions, or even hundreds of billions, of stars and planets, clustered together in a distinct shape, like a spiral or ellipse. Our Earth is located within the Milky Way Galaxy.

GENRE
A type, or kind, or a work of art. In literature, a genre is distinguished by a common subject, theme, or style. Some genres include science fiction, fantasy, and mystery.

INTERGALACTIC

Something that happens or exists between two or more galaxies.

INTERSTELLAR

Something that happens or exists between the stars of a galaxy. A rocketship that travels through interstellar space is moving from one star system to the next.

PROTAGONIST

The main character in a story, usually the hero.

SPACE OPERA

A type of science fiction that emphasizes strong characters, a sense of wonder, and non-stop action and adventure. *Star Wars* is a good example of modern space opera. Space opera usually takes place on distant planets, featuring spaceships that can quickly travel between the stars. The term was probably coined in 1941 by author Wilson Tucker, as a play on the terms "horse opera" (Westerns) and "soap opera."

UTOPIA

A utopia is an imaginary place where everything is perfect. The name comes from the book *Utopia*, written in 1516 by Sir Thomas More, about a fictional island and its seemingly perfect society. In a utopia, people are equal, nobody's poor, there is no war, and everybody gets along. The word utopia is a combination of two Greek words, *ou* and *topos*. Put together, it literally means "nowhere," or "no-place." A utopia is an ideal, a place that doesn't really exist—but everyone wishes it did.

INDEX